America's
ANIMAL
COMEBACKS

California Condors

Saved by Captive Breeding

by Meish Goldish

Consultant: Sanford Wilbur
U.S. Fish and Wildlife Service (retired)
Condor Research and Recovery Team Leader 1969–1981

BEARPORT
PUBLISHING

New York, New York

Credits

Cover and Title Page, © Studio Carlo Dani/Animals Animals Enterprises; 4, © John McNeely/U.S. Fish and Wildlife Sevice; 5, © R.& N. Bowers/VIREO; 6, © American Museum of Natural History; 7, © AP Images/Mark J. Terrill; 8, © David Clendenen/ U.S. Fish and Wildlife Sevice; 9, © The Field Museum; 11L, © Rich Reid/National Geographic/Getty Images; 11R, © Museum of Vertebrate Zoology; 13, © John Brooks/ U.S. Fish and Wildlife Sevice; 14, © Ron Garrison/Zoological Society of San Diego; 15, © Joel Sartore Photography; 16, © John Brooks/U.S. Fish and Wildlife Sevice; 17, © Ron Garrison/Zoological Society of San Diego; 18L, © F.D. Schmidt/Zoological Society of San Diego; 18R, © Ron Garrison/Zoological Society of San Diego/U.S. Fish and Wildlife Sevice; 19, © Ron Garrison/Zoological Society of San Diego/U.S. Fish and Wildlife Sevice; 20, © zumaphotos/newscom; 20-21, © C. Van Cleve/VIREO; 21, © Photodisc/ SuperStock; 22-23, © AP Images/Ben Margot; 24, © AP Images/Mark J. Terrill; 24-25, © AP Images/Spencer Weiner; 26, © Zoological Society of San Diego; 27, © C. Van Cleve/ VIREO; 28, © David Clendenen/U.S. Fish and Wildlife Sevice; 29T, © Hinrich Baeseman/ dpaphotos/newscom; 29B, © Winfried Wisniewski/Foto Natura/Minden Pictures; 31, © Kelly Biesen; 32, © United States Treasury Department.

Publisher: Kenn Goin
Editorial Director: Adam Siegel
Creative Director: Spencer Brinker
Photo Researcher: Michael Fergenson
Cover Design: Dawn Beard Creative

Library of Congress Cataloging-in-Publication Data

Goldish, Meish.
  California condors : saved by captive breeding / by Meish Goldish.
      p. cm. — (America's animal comebacks)
  Includes bibliographical references and index.
  ISBN-13: 978-1-59716-741-3 (library binding)
  ISBN-10: 1-59716-741-X (library binding)
  1. California condor—Conservation—United States—Juvenile literature. 2. California condor—Reintroduction—United States—Juvenile literature. I. Title.

  QL696.C53G65 2009
  598.9'2—dc22

                              2008032803

For more information, write to Bearport Publishing Company, Inc., 101 Fifth Avenue, Suite 6R, New York, New York, 10003. Printed in the United States of America.

10 9 8 7 6 5 4 3 2 1

Contents

The Last Wild Condor

On April 19, 1987, a California condor named AC-9 soared high in the sky. The bird spotted a dead calf on the ground below. He flew down to eat some of the meat. Suddenly, **biologists** hiding nearby fired a net from a big gun, trapping the large bird. The last wild California condor in the world had just been captured.

AC-9 being captured

Scientists use codes to identify California condors. AC-9 stands for Adult Condor Number Nine.

The scientists were filled with hope and excitement. They knew that California condors had been dying out for years. Soon the birds might be **extinct**. Their only chance to save the condors was to capture them and **breed** them in zoos. Then they could try to **release** the **chicks** back into the wild. With AC-9, scientists had finally captured all the wild condors—but there were only 27 in all. Would they be enough to save the **species**?

The California condor is the largest bird in North America.

A Free Life

California condors once enjoyed a life of freedom in North America. Forty thousand years ago, the birds soared over large parts of the west and southwest, including California, Texas, New Mexico, and Arizona. They fed on prehistoric animals such as giant sloths, ancient bison, and camels.

This painting shows a prehistoric condor trying to eat a dead camel.

About 10,000 years ago, however, the **climate** of the southwest became more desert-like. Most of the animals that the condor ate died out. To find food, condors in the southwest were forced to move farther west, near the Pacific Ocean. The climate there was milder. There were also many animals that the condor could eat. The large black birds were able to feed on whales, sea lions, pronghorn antelope, deer, and elk.

Native Americans who lived near the condors in California and Oregon respected the bird. The condor appears in many of their **myths** and **legends**. Feathers from the bird were also used in their religious ceremonies.

This Native American holds condor feathers during his prayer.

Trouble Starts

In the late 1800s, life for condors became more difficult. Many people from Europe were **settling** across America. In the west, they sometimes shot the large black birds flying in the sky just for fun.

Other condors died from eating poisoned meat that ranchers had left out for coyotes and bears. The ranchers hoped to protect their **livestock** by killing these wild animals. Unfortunately, condors also ate the poisoned meat and died.

Condors are a type of vulture—a bird that finds food by searching for dead animals. California condors do not hunt and kill living animals.

By the 1940s, the condor **population** was very small—only about 150. As the birds became **rare**, they also became more valuable to collectors. Museums paid people to bring them condors and their eggs. As a result, even fewer of the birds were left in the wild.

Many people killed condors so that they could sell them for museum displays, such as this one.

In the 1940s, California condors no longer lived all across the western coast of North America. Instead, they could be found in just a small part of California.

Studying the Problem

From 1939 to 1946, a scientist named Carl Koford studied the California condor. He saw how the birds lived and behaved. He watched how they fed, traveled, and bred. From his studies, Koford could see that the birds lived in a very small area of California—and that they were close to dying out.

California Condors in the Wild

☐ Where California condors lived 10,000 years ago
■ Where California condors lived in the 1940s

Koford's research convinced **wildlife officials** that condors needed a safe place to live. In 1947, they created the Sespe Condor **Sanctuary** in California's Los Padres National Forest. Condors that lived in its 35,000 acres (14,164 hectares) were safe from hunters. Unfortunately, this was not enough to save them. There were so few birds left that it was hard for them to increase their numbers.

Carl Koford

In 1951, the Sespe Condor Sanctuary was expanded to 53,000 acres (21,448 hectares).

A New Plan

In 1953, California passed a law that made it illegal to "take any condor at any time or in any manner." More laws were passed in the 1960s and 1970s to help protect the birds. Yet the population continued to get smaller. In 1967, there were only about 50 to 60 California condors left. By 1979, only about 30 were still alive. To save them from dying out, wildlife officials came up with a new idea. They planned to capture wild condors and breed them in **captivity**.

Condors in California

Area where California condors lived in the 1940s

Where California condors lived in the 1980s

This map shows how the area where California condors lived got smaller between 1940 and 1980.

Not everyone thought the idea was a good one. Some scientists feared that handling the birds would harm or kill them. Others believed that condors kept in zoos wouldn't breed. Yet many biologists thought that if they did nothing, the California condor would soon become extinct. So with time running out, the scientists began preparing to capture the birds.

In the wild, California condors lay their eggs in cliffs and in caves. Some scientists thought that if the birds were kept in zoos they wouldn't lay eggs anymore.

In 1975, the California Condor Recovery Team was formed. Members of the team work to find the best ways to protect California condors and help their population grow.

Special Homes

Wildlife officials knew they needed places to breed and raise the California condors that they hoped to catch. So the San Diego Zoo's Wild Animal Park and the Los Angeles Zoo built large screened pens where the birds could safely live. The new homes were called condorminiums.

A condorminium at the San Diego Zoo's Wild Animal Park

Each condorminium was built to house a pair of mating condors. It had feeding areas for the birds, plus ponds for drinking and bathing. There were poles where the condors could **perch** and nest boxes so the birds could **roost**. Scientists placed TV cameras in some places so they could watch how the birds behaved.

Condorminiums have screened-off areas where people can watch the condors without disturbing them.

An "Egg-cellent" Plan

Scientists first began to capture California condors in 1982. At that time, they took only chicks to raise at the zoos. They left the adult birds in the wild so that they would lay more eggs.

A female condor usually lays only one egg every other year, so it is hard for condors to increase their population when just a few of them are left. However, scientists discovered a clever way to make the birds lay more eggs.

Scientists handle condor eggs carefully in order not to damage them.

Scientists had noticed that when a condor egg is lost, the mother lays a second one to replace it. If that egg is lost, often a third egg is laid. As a result, scientists took condor eggs from the wild so that the parents would produce more. They brought the eggs back to the zoos, where they hoped to **hatch** them in captivity.

A scientist watching an egg being incubated at the San Diego Zoo.

Wild condor eggs were **incubated** at the zoos. Special machines kept each egg warm so the chick inside could develop safely.

New Arrivals

In March 1983, the scientists had their first big success. A condor egg from the wild hatched at the San Diego Zoo. The chick was named Sisquoc. It was fed by a person wearing a hand puppet. The puppet looked like an adult condor because scientists wanted the chick to think its parents—not humans—were caring for it.

Sisquoc, just 12 hours old

A condor chick being fed by a hand puppet

Soon, more condor chicks hatched at the zoos. Unfortunately, the adult birds in the wild were still dying out. By 1985, there were only nine condors left in the wild. Soon there might be none!

Over the next two years, scientists rescued the last wild condors. Yet one key question remained. Would the birds lay eggs in captivity? It didn't take long for scientists to get their answer. In 1988, an egg was laid at the San Diego Zoo. It hatched on April 29, and Molloko was born!

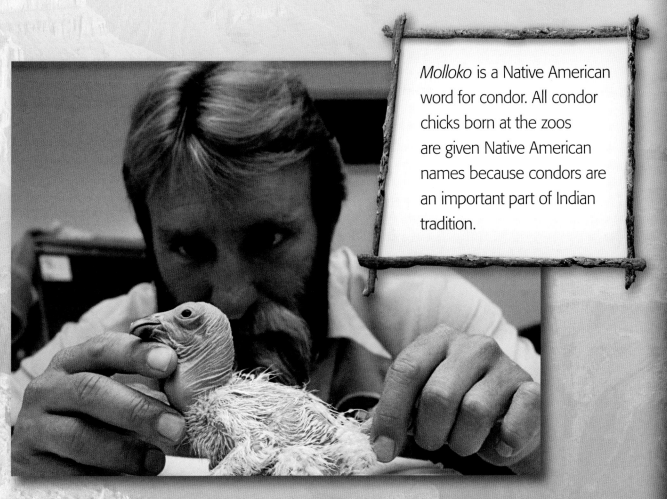

Molloko is a Native American word for condor. All condor chicks born at the zoos are given Native American names because condors are an important part of Indian tradition.

Molloko's birth proved that California condors would lay eggs in captivity.

Return to the Wild

The captive breeding plan seemed to be working. By 1992, 52 California condors lived in the two zoos. Scientists decided it was time to take the next step. On January 14, 1992, they released two of the birds into the wild. Would they survive on their own? At first everything seemed to be going well. Yet in October, one of the birds drank some **antifreeze** and died.

Officials put numbers and **radio transmitters** on all California condors before releasing them into the wild. That way, they can track each bird.

This scientist is using a radio transmitter to track condors.

Scientists released six more condors in December. Unlike wild birds, however, the condors raised in zoos were used to being around people. As a result, they often got into trouble. When some of the condors saw hikers coming near, they attacked their shoelaces. Others tore through the screen door of a person's home, ripped windshield wipers from trucks, and pulled tents apart. Sadly, three of the condors sat on power poles and were **electrocuted**.

Power lines turned deadly for California condors when they touched the powerful electric wires.

radio transmitter

Necessary Changes

Scientists realized that they needed to make changes to their breeding program. Captive condors had to learn how to stay away from people—and power poles. So scientists added fake power poles to the condorminiums. If a bird landed on a pole, it received a small shock. The condor wasn't hurt, but it learned not to sit there again.

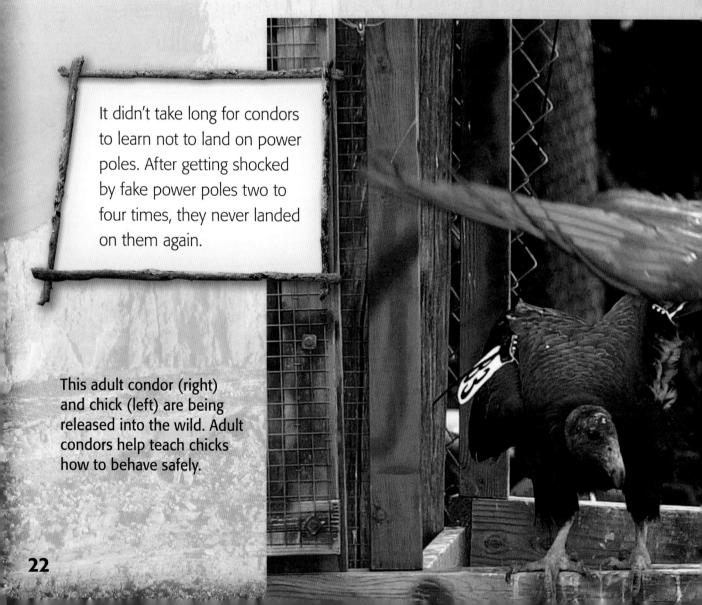

It didn't take long for condors to learn not to land on power poles. After getting shocked by fake power poles two to four times, they never landed on them again.

This adult condor (right) and chick (left) are being released into the wild. Adult condors help teach chicks how to behave safely.

Scientists also taught condors to fear people. They would rush toward the birds, catch them, and place them in cages. The condors were released only at night. Since the birds didn't want to be kept in cages, over time they learned to stay away from humans.

With the new training, more California condors were set free in the wild. This time, they stayed away from people and power poles. The birds survived—and they laid eggs.

Growing Numbers

In 2002, a historic event took place. AC-9, the last condor that had been captured, was released back into the wild. It had been 15 years since his rescue. He was now 22 years old. After he was released, he became the father of several chicks.

A crowd gathered to watch AC-9 being released into the wild.

The California condor breeding program has turned out to be a huge success. Today, about 320 California condors live in the western United States and Mexico. About half of those birds live in the wild. The rest are kept in breeding centers. Some captive condors are cared for at the zoos in California. Others live in two newer breeding centers in Oregon and Idaho.

Today, many California condors are released near the Grand Canyon in Arizona, and in Baja California, Mexico.

AC-9 taking his first flight in the wild after 15 years of captivity

The Future

Wildlife officials are pleased by the growing number of California condors. Their goal is to have at least 300 birds in the wild, plus 150 in captivity. The number of condors keeps increasing. Yet the birds still face serious problems. Some die because they eat animals shot by hunters. When condors eat the meat they also swallow small pieces of the lead bullets, which poison them. Other condors die or get sick from trash that they swallow.

Some condors died after eating bottle caps, broken glass, and metal washers that had been left near the places where the birds lived.

Luckily, a new law was passed in California in 2007. Hunters must now use lead-free bullets in places where condors live. Scientists are also teaching condors to keep away from trash. Biologists at the San Diego Zoo have wired pieces of trash so that they give small shocks, like those from fake power poles. Hopefully, the birds will learn to stay away from garbage. If these efforts succeed, California condors will continue to soar proudly over North America.

Scientists want to have two separate condor populations in the wild—one in California and one in Arizona. They are hoping for at least 150 wild condors in each state.

California Condor Facts

In 1973, Congress passed the **Endangered** Species Act. This law protects animals and plants that are in danger of dying out in the United States. Harmful activities, such as hunting, capturing, or collecting endangered species, are illegal under this act.

The California condor was one of the first species listed under the Endangered Species Act. Here are some other facts about this bird.

Population

1600: unknown, but fairly common   **1987**: 27

1940s: about 150   **Today:** about 320

Weight	Wingspan	Length
17–25 pounds (7.7–11.3 kg)	about 9.5 feet (2.9 m)	43–55 inches (1.1–1.4 m)

Colors

Adult condors: black body; gray head and neck with shades of yellow, red, and orange

Young condors: gray body; gray head and neck with shades of pink

Food	Life Span	Habitat
dead animals, including deer, cows, sheep, rabbits, and rodents	up to 60 years	California, Arizona, and Mexico

Other Vultures in Danger

The California condor is one kind of vulture that's making a comeback by increasing its numbers. Other types of vultures are also trying to make a comeback.

Andean Condor

- The Andean condor is the largest kind of condor. Its wingspan is about 10.5 feet (3 m) wide.

- It is estimated that there are a few thousand Andean condors still alive. They live in South America.

- The Andean condor is the national symbol of Colombia. The bird appears on the country's coins and paper money.

- Breeding programs at zoos in North America and South America are helping Andean condors make a comeback.

Bearded Vulture

- Bearded vultures live in parts of Europe, Africa, and Asia. The birds are endangered in Europe— only about 200 of them exist there.

- Bearded vultures eat mostly the bones of dead animals.

- Programs in Europe to protect bearded vulture eggs and chicks are helping these birds make a comeback.

Glossary

antifreeze (AN-ti-*freez*) a substance that lowers the freezing point of a liquid

biologists (bye-OL-uh-jists) scientists who study animals or plants

breed (BREED) keeping animals so that they can mate and produce young

captivity (kap-TIV-uh-tee) places where animals live in which they are cared for by people, and which are not the animals' natural environments

chicks (CHIKS) baby birds

climate (KLYE-mit) the typical weather in a place

electrocuted (i-LEK-truh-*kyoot*-id) killed by a strong electric shock

endangered (en-DAYN-jurd) in danger of dying out completely

extinct (ek-STINGKT) when a kind of plant or animal has died out; no more of its kind is living anywhere in the world

hatch (HACH) to bring forth a baby from an egg

incubated (ING-kyuh-*bayt*-id) kept an egg warm so that the baby inside could develop and hatch

legends (LEJ-uhndz) stories handed down from long ago that are often based on some facts but cannot be proven true

livestock (LIVE-*stok*) animals, such as cows and sheep, that are raised by people on farms or ranches

myths (MITHS) traditional stories that often tell of larger-than-life beings and mysterious events

perch (PURCH) to sit or stand on the edge of something

population (*pop*-yuh-LAY-shuhn) the number of people or animals living in a place

radio transmitters (RAY-dee-oh TRANZ-mit-urz) objects that send out radio signals and are put on animals so that their movements can be tracked

rare (RAIR) not often found or seen

release (ri-LEESS) to set free

roost (ROOST) to rest in a nest

sanctuary (SANGK-choo-*er*-ee) an area where animals are protected from hunters and can live safely

settling (SET-ling) living or making a home in a new place

species (SPEE-sheez) groups that animals are divided into, according to similar characteristics; members of the same species can have offspring together

wildlife officials (WILDE-*life* uh-FISH-uhlz) people whose job is to study and protect wild animals

Bibliography

Nielsen, John. *Condor: To the Brink and Back—The Life and Times of One Giant Bird.* New York: HarperCollins (2006).

Snyder, Noel and Helen. *The California Condor: A Saga of Natural History and Conservation.* San Diego: Academic Press (2000).

cacondorconservation.org (California Condor Conservation)

conservationandscience.org/projects/sp_condors_recovery_program .html (California Condor Recovery Program)

cres.sandiegozoo.org/projects/sp_condors_milestones.html (Milestones in California Condor Conservation)

Read More

Graves, Bonnie B. *California Condor: Flying Free.* Logan, IA: Perfection Learning (2002).

Imbriaco, Alison. *The California Condor: Help Save This Endangered Species!* Berkeley Heights, NJ: Enslow Publishers (2007).

Miller-Schroeder, Patricia, and Susan Ring. *California Condors.* Chicago: Raintree (2004).

Povey, Karen D. *The Condor.* San Diego: Lucent Books (2001).

Learn More Online

To learn more about California condors, visit
www.bearportpublishing.com/AnimalComebacks

Index

About the Author

Meish Goldish has written more than 100 books for children. His books *Florida Manatees: Warm Water Miracles* and *Gray Wolves: Return to Yellowstone* were recommended by the National Science Teachers Association in 2008.